CW00726493

from confetti.co.uk
don't get married without us...

First published in 2001 by Octopus Publishing Group,
2–4 Heron Quays, London, E14 4JP
www.conran-octopus.co.uk

ISBN 1 84091 226 X

Publishing Director Lorraine Dickey;
Creative Director Leslie Harrington;
Senior Editor Katey Day; *Copy-editor* Helen Ridge;
Designer Megan Smith; *Production Director* Zoë Fawcett

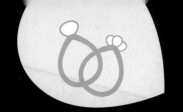

Contents

Is it written in the stars that you should be together? Perhaps the secret is in the palm of your hand. Or maybe it's to do with your body shapes. Hang on – could it be which Chinese Year you were born in? Or does your date of birth have the numerological answer?

INTRODUCTION

Confetti.co.uk has helped thousands of compatible couples down the aisle, and now we bring together six different methods for assessing your compatibility together with full results.

And if your handwriting tells you your destiny is together forever, then check out confetti.co.uk for help with the next step!

Astro-love...

Can a fiery Sagittarian live with a down-to-earth Capricorn? Will an airy Gemini get blown away by a watery Scorpio? Work out your astrological element, then read on for your star compatibility.

EARTH = Capricorn, Taurus, Virgo
AIR = Aquarius, Gemini, Libra
FIRE = Aries, Leo, Sagittarius
WATER = Pisces, Cancer, Scorpio

Earth (female) + Water (male)

Sex and spirituality are strong in this twosome. He can be moody, but you're able to laugh it off – ha! You bring in the cash, keep a calm home and are super-practical. No wonder he's a happy bunny…

Earth (female) + Air (male)

You like to play it safe and bring sanity to the relationship, while he has the gift of the gab and the social skills to go with it – which all adds up to a fun pairing.

Earth (female) + Fire (male)

Every day is a celebration with this fire sign
– he rounds up the guests, you organize the
booze. Together you can climb mountains,
but hang on to the rope 'cos you tend to
travel at different speeds…

Earth (female) + Earth (male)
The earth will certainly move for you as
this is one of the most harmonious
matches you can get. You know exactly
what makes each other tick and how to
press all the right buttons!

Air (female) + Water (male)

You're both gentle, sensitive souls – but
in totally different ways. Appreciate each
other's views and you'll share a special
kind of love.

Air (female) + Air (male)

You two are real chatterboxes and once you start, there's no stopping you. Practical you're not, but who cares when the conversation's this good?

Air (female) + Fire (male)

Whoa! People can feel the energy between you two – and it's hot! Just try to calm it down occasionally to avoid burn-out.

Air (female) + Earth (male)

He's your rock, and you love him for the way he grounds you. In return for his warmth and security, teach him to chill out a little and take some chances.

Fire (female) + Water (male)

Others find your relationship inscrutable,
but you both get it. You love the air
of intrigue about him, while he's inspired
by your optimism.

Fire (female) + Air (male)

He'll fan your flames, giving your ideas the chance to become bigger, better and bolder. And if that isn't enough, he'll cheer you up when you're down.

Fire (female) + Fire (male)

Phew, what a scorcher! Your love life is a hotbed of events and emotions, and you're brimming with excitement. Too hot to handle? Definitely not for you two.

Fire (female) + Earth (male)
There'll be highs and lows – but that's what makes this pairing work. You provide the fiery optimism, while he keeps your relationship cool, calm and collected.

Water (female) + Water (male)
You two are so deep, but there's no chance of this relationship drowning. You're both sensitive and intuitive, and your powerful telepathy means you don't always need to talk.

Water (female) + Air (male)

You're both quirky – and you love each other for your funny little ways. Combine that with your powers of perception and this is a relationship that's here to stay.

Water (female) + Fire (male)
You'd do anything to protect your
partner, and he adores you for it. In return,
he'll help you realize your dreams and lead
you on to new adventures...

Water (female) + Earth (male)

You help bring his emotions to the surface and stop him getting bogged down with life's boring bits. And him? He'll help you to unravel life's mysteries and provide all the romance a girl could need…

Living by numbers

Have you got your partner's number?

In numerology, the most significant number is the one that relates to your date of birth, and comparing your number with your partner's can tell you a great deal about your compatibility.

To work out your key number, write down your date of birth, then add all the single numbers together in that date until you arrive at a single digit.

For example, if your birth date is 12/7/1970: 1+2+7+1+9+7+0 = 27

2+7 = **NINE** = your key number

How the numbers work

In assessing compatibility, the numbers work both ways for couples. So, if you're a **TWO** and your partner's a **THREE**, the combination is the same as if you were the **THREE** and your partner the **TWO**. Now read on to see what the numbers reveal about your compatibility.

One + One

ONEs always love to take the lead,
which, with both of you the same
number, can lead to a clash of egos.
This may result in a volatile pairing but,
because you both recognize a bit of
yourself in the other, you're always quick
to kiss and make up.

One + Two

Because **ONE**s love to organize and
be the queen bee, **TWO**s make
perfect mates because of their
cooperative and adaptable nature –
they know how to let their partner feel
as if they're in the driving seat (even
when they're not!).

1 + 2

One + Three

Communicative and creative **THREE**s bring out the pioneering and equally creative nature of **ONE**s, so between chats and projects, there's never a dull moment in this pairing.

One + Four

ONEs are great at organizing others and
FOURs are eminently practical. So, if
anything needs doing around the house, it'll
be **FOUR** who actually gets the job done.

One + Five

Self-reliant **ONE**s make great mates for **FIVE**s, whose tendency to work in jobs related to the arts often leaves their partners with time on their hands.

One + Six

Even those who are born to lead, like
ONEs, need to feel loved, so a pairing
with a compassionate and caring **SIX** is
an ideal combination – especially as **SIX**es
go all soft inside over their partner's
strong personality!

One + Seven

ONE's managerial and creative skills
help to bring sensitive and introspective
SEVENs out of their shells, while
sensitive **SEVEN**s help to soften **ONE**'s
sharper edges. A good emotional and
intellectual blend.

One + Eight

EIGHT's organizational skills and bold ambition are the perfect foil for **ONE**'s equally forceful nature. This is a partnership built on mutual ambition that will go from strength to strength.

One + Nine

ONEs are leaders, while **NINE**s are teachers – this is a textbook case of opposites attracting. Celebrate your differences as they are the bedrock of your relationship.

Two + Two

Great diplomats, gentle and adaptable
TWOs together are highly compatible.
This is a partnership based on mutual
respect, and because you're great
peacemakers, you'll never go to sleep
on an argument.

Two + Three

Enthusiastic and optimistic, high-spirited **THREE**s make a great match for sensitive **TWO**s, who can sometimes be slightly melancholic. However, **TWO**'s naturally diplomatic nature helps to alleviate **THREE**'s tendency to worry.

2 + 3

Two + Four

This pairing will run and run as **TWO**'s
adaptable and tension-busting nature suits
FOUR's occasional over-the-top sense
of responsibility and slight resistance
to change.

Two + Five

TWOs are the great mediators, while
FIVEs are the great communicators,
so you are evenly matched in this
relationship. The union is further helped
by **TWO**'s cautious nature, which
helps balance out **FIVE**'s sometimes
unfocused energy.

Two + Six

This is a happy, well-balanced mix.
TWOs are always keen to see both sides
of an argument, while **SIX**'s caring nature
means that you will always be happy to
support each other and help each other
to develop.

Two + Seven

You're both self-reliant, so this is a
partnership built on respect for each
other's need for personal space. As a result,
the times you spend together are even
more special – just make sure you make
the most of them!

Two + Eight

TWOs and **EIGHT**s are born planners and organizers, which means they complement one another well. The two of you know exactly where you're heading – and exactly what you need to do to get there.

Two + Nine

This is a partnership made in heaven. While **NINE** represents leadership and creativity, **TWO**s are born diplomats and peacemakers, who are well able to handle the feisty side of their partner's personality.

Three + Three

THREE represents optimism, originality and connection. Self-expression is very important to **THREE**s, who are often artists and writers, so in this relationship the flights of fancy are never far away!

Three + Four

While **THREE** represents self-expression and extravagance, **FOUR**s are builder types – solid and practical. So, **THREE** brings energy and playfulness to the relationship, while **FOUR** is the responsible one who reminds you to pay your credit card bills after the fun has been had!

Three + Five

With both **THREE**s and **FIVE**s drawn to careers in the media and arts, this is a partnership built on passion and parties. You're both prone to extravagance and over-indulgence — so set your boundaries and stick to them!

Three + Six

The numbers **THREE** and **SIX** are both strongly linked with feelings and emotions. Sensitive **THREE**s are drawn to loving and compassionate **SIX**es, which makes for a contented, if sometimes emotionally charged, home life.

3 + 6

Three + Seven

THREEs — free spirits and original thinkers that they are — are well paired with **SEVEN**s, who are inclined to be introspective and perfectionist types. **THREE** makes sure that **SEVEN** takes life less seriously, while **SEVEN** helps to cool down **THREE**, who can have a bit of a sharp tongue at times!

Three + Eight

Although **THREE** and **EIGHT** both bring
a powerful energy to their relationship,
this is a real case of opposites attracting:
THREEs love the passion and drive that
fuel their mate's analytical mind, while
EIGHTs are suckers for original-thinking,
creative **THREE**s.

Three + Nine

THREEs and **NINE**s are both creative and quick-thinking. Self-contained **NINE** has a balancing effect on **THREE**'s sometimes flighty nature. On the other hand, **NINE**s can occasionally become a little too serious, and **THREE**s help them to lighten up.

Four + Four

Practical, down-to-earth **FOUR**s set great store by strong moral values and a sense of responsibility. Naturally, they look for this in their partners, so hooking up with another **FOUR** makes for a solid relationship that's built to last.

Four + Five

FOURs are practical and energetic, which makes them the perfect accompaniment for **FIVE**s, the talkers and thinkers. While **FOUR**s get on with putting up shelves and stripping wallpaper, **FIVE**s will take control of colour schemes and budgets.

4 + 5

Four + Six

Hard-working and dependable **FOUR**s
are ideally suited to caring, compassionate
SIXes – when **FOUR** returns home after a
long day at work, **SIX** is quick to make sure
they rest and recuperate. All in all,
this pairing bodes well for a long-lasting,
loving and stable partnership.

Four + Seven

Practical and responsible **FOUR**s offer great partnership potential to sensitive and spiritual **SEVEN**s, especially as you're both modest and enjoy helping others. You make a serious-minded couple – just make sure you take time to enjoy the lighter side of life, too!

Four + Eight

This is a peach of a partnership! **FOUR**s
like to plan projects and get their
hands dirty, while **EIGHT**s prefer to stand
back and organize the show. You both
have a tendency to be stubborn but, luckily,
it is rarely about the same things.
Fortunately, if one of you decides to dig
your heels in about something, the other is
usually willing to compromise.

Four + Nine

Down-to-earth **FOUR**s make good mates
for creative and imaginative **NINE**s.
FOUR brings stability to the relationship,
while **NINE** offers leadership. Your different
perspectives on life enrich and strengthen
the bond between you.

Five + Five

FIVEs are great communicators and thinkers, debaters and generators of ideas. You make a charismatic couple and thrive in careers of a creative bent, which means you both understand the demands each other faces at work. And if ever you work on a project together, the results are sure to be spectacular!

Five + Six

A sweet pairing. **FIVE**s tend to enter relationships on an intellectual level, reasoning their way into a relationship, while caring **SIX**es are soppier, more emotional creatures. **SIX**es are very touchy-feely and will always want to hug and make up after a fight – something that will make perfect sense to a **FIVE**.

Five + Seven

Outgoing, talkative **FIVE**s are great partners for sensitive and introspective **SEVEN**s, because they know how to bring them out of their shells. **SEVEN**s tend to be modest and steady, and are usually happy to let their partner take centre stage in the relationship.

Five + Eight

Communicative **FIVE**s do well with **EIGHT**s, because their clear-sighted, well-ordered minds are a great foil for the passionate maelstrom that's bubbling away in **EIGHT**'s head! Your happiness centres on the plans you lay together; you have the capacity to inspire each other to be the best you can be.

Five + Nine

Although this tends to be an unusual combination, **FIVE**s and **NINE**s get on like a house on fire because both have artistic, intellectual leanings. This numerological combination has a strong influence on the mind, which means you're both likely to be drawn to careers that use your intellect, such as teaching or medicine.

Six + Six

SIXes are loving and compassionate partners. When they come together in a relationship, they form *the* archetypal romantic couple, forever kissing and cuddling, and unable to walk down the street without holding hands.

Six + Seven

Couples that are all **SIX**es and **SEVEN**s
function superbly together. **SEVEN**s like
to look after their **SIX**es, and make sure
that they get the best in all things, which
reassures their partner – who can
sometimes need a little convincing on
the subject – that they are well and
truly cherished.

Six + Eight

SIXes, kind-hearted and full of good intentions, sit nicely next to **EIGHT**s, who are efficient and practical types. **SIX**es are great ones for buying little unexpected gifts to show their partner they care, while **EIGHT**s look after the finances and make sure there's always food on the table!

Six + Nine

Though this is quite an unusual combination of numbers, it can frequently work wonders, as **SIX**'s warm, loving nature melts **NINE**'s legendary self-control. And **NINE**s – great ones for taking charge in a crisis – give the relationship structure and direction.

Seven + Seven

When two perfectionists get together, watch out – you can appear a little eccentric to those around you. But you're both sensitive, introspective and modest, and you place great value on the spiritual side of your lives. A profoundly compatible coupling!

Seven + Eight

Viewed from the outside, it might easily look as if energetic **EIGHT** runs the show in this love match. But, in fact, **EIGHT**s adore their gentle partners and will do everything in their power to please them. Meanwhile, **SEVEN**s, with their eye for the things that really matter in life and love, quietly take the edge off their partner's well-developed materialistic side.

Seven + Nine

SEVEN and **NINE** make for a spiritual, even mystical, pairing. You both believe in signs and wonders, and are convinced that fate meant you to be together. There's something almost otherworldly about the attraction between you!

Eight + Eight

An **EIGHT** is a person who likes to get off their backside and make things happen, so a double-**EIGHT** is a dynamic duo. You're both ambitious and have a natural flair for business. Just don't forget to make time for yourselves and simply relax and play!

8+8

Eight + Nine

EIGHTs and **NINE**s are both powerful personalities – go-ahead types who like to be in the driving seat. This is a volatile combination and sparks will fly, as **NINE**s can be as headstrong as **EIGHT**s are stubborn. Then again, there's rarely a dull moment between you!

Nine + Nine

When **NINE**s get together, their humanitarian, idealistic sides come to the fore and a sure, deep bond is guaranteed. You like to help out others and support causes together, and you're in your element making thoughtful, long-term plans for your lives together.

What your body says about you

According to the Chinese art of body reading, your personality, where you are in life and what you want from relationships are connected to your body build. There are five basic body shapes: thin and wiry; tall and rangy; fleshy and well rounded; stocky; and medium build. Each type corresponds to one of the five elements: **FIRE**, **WOOD**, **GOLD**, **EARTH**, **WATER**. Now see what your body type and your partner's say about your relationship.

COMPATIBILITY

What's your body type?
1. Tall and rangy = **WOOD**
(e.g. Jerry Hall, Jarvis Cocker)
2. Fleshy and well rounded = **WATER**
(e.g. Marilyn Monroe, Elton John)
3. Thin and wiry = **FIRE**
(e.g. Victoria Beckham, Brad Pitt)
4. Stocky = **EARTH**
(e.g. Ricki Lake, Bob Hoskins)
5. Medium build = **GOLD**
(e.g. Jennifer Lopez, Leonardo DiCaprio)

Wood + Wood

Great dreamers and drifters, **WOOD** personalities like to bond intellectually before getting physically involved. Once in love, **WOOD** types tend to be great romantics, and their love burns slow and strong...

Wood + Water

WOOD types are deep thinkers and great conversationalists. They make loyal, lifelong companions, and so are a great match for **WATER** types, for whom family, a stable marriage and lots of kids are always top priority.

Wood + Fire

In this elemental mix, the analytical
WOOD character provides a happy
balancing force for **FIRE**-types, who are
usually brimming over with physical energy.
FIRE-types are exciting lovers, and with
WOOD they make the perfect combination
to keep passion aflame.

Wood + Earth

EARTH-types are great listeners, so they sit pretty next to chatty, daydreamy **WOOD**-types. **EARTH** listens to **WOOD**'s grand schemes, while keeping their feet planted firmly on the ground. In return, **WOOD** provides **EARTH** with the imaginative flair to bring their careful plans to life.

Wood + Gold

GOLD-types are born managers and organizers, who love to socialize, especially at events of their own devising. They are a great match for **WOOD**-types who, left to their own devices, would quite happily drift off into their own little fantasy world!

Water + Water

Adaptable and quick-witted, **WATER**-types tend to be charming, seductive and warm-hearted. While you both like to get your own way, you also love to please your partner — and you tend to be romantic and generous lovers. Enjoy each other!

Water + Fire

Great conversationalists and vocal about their emotions, **WATER**-types are well suited to **FIRE**-types, who are also stimulating conversationalists. Financially, you're well matched as you're both great entrepreneurs — **WATER**-types, in particular, enjoy making money!

Water + Earth

EARTH-types really know how to listen, so they complement chatty **WATER**-types admirably. Solid, dependable and very hard-working, they provide down-to-**EARTH** security and a stable home for **WATER** boys and girls, who are equally family-loving.

Water + Gold

Both **WATER**- and **GOLD**-types love to
paint the town red – you're the couple who
are the life and soul of every party,
so you're never short of invitations.
But while **GOLD**-types enjoy playing
sports, **WATER**-types are happy to
support their partner from the stands
by applauding enthusiastically!

Fire + Fire

It won't surprise you that this is a truly combustible combination. **FIRE**-types often appear restless and are forever on the move. This is great because you can both share your love of travel and finding new places. Bon voyage!

Fire + Earth

Roaming **FIRE**-types and solid **EARTH**-types do well together as **FIRE** brings a little adventure into **EARTH**'s life, while **EARTH** provides stability and security in **FIRE**'s unending quest for new experiences. You've got a lot to offer each other!

Fire + Gold

FIRE- and **GOLD**-types both love to get out and meet new people, socialize and play sports, though when it comes to sports, competitive **FIRE** tends to win. **FIRE**-types are red-hot lovers, while **GOLD**s, though more reserved and slow-burning when it comes to sex, are no slouches in bed either. Time to make whoopee!

Earth + Earth

EARTH-types very often find themselves hitching up with **EARTH**-types as you're both essentially home-birds and like nothing better than a quiet night, relaxing in front of the television. You're likely to share other similar values, especially a belief in good old-fashioned hard work, and a strong desire to have a family.

Earth + Gold

Hard-working, home-loving **EARTH**-types like to hang out with outgoing, extrovert **GOLD**-types. In such a pairing, **EARTH** gives **GOLD** security and focus, while **GOLD** offers **EARTH** a chance to broaden their horizons.

Gold + Gold

Bold **GOLD**-types are ambitious high-flyers who love the good things in life and are prepared to pay what it takes for the best: you especially share a love of travel and beautiful clothes. Well travelled and sometimes restless, you may take a while to choose your partner and settle down, but when you do, it's for life!

Palmistry

It's in your hands...

In palmistry, the shape of your hands reveals a great deal about the kind of person you are. There are four basic shapes:

SQUARE: Wide, square palm with few deep lines; coarse skin; short, square-tipped fingers.

PHILOSOPHICAL: Square, short palms; fine, dry skin; long, broad, round-tipped fingers.

SPATULATE: Thick, oblong palms; springy skin; short fingers.

CONIC: Long, thin, oblong palms; fine skin; narrow, tapering fingers.

Square + Square

Practical and down-to-earth **SQUARE**s often seek out equally down-to-earth partners, so this is a great combination. You both love food and drink and getting out and about in the countryside – romantic weekend breaks are made for you!

Square + Philosophical

Cautious **SQUARE**s and quick-witted **PHILOSOPHICAL**s go together to form a well-balanced relationship. While **SQUARE**s are good at dealing with the practicalities of daily life, **PHILOSOPHICAL**s will ensure that you don't forget to have some fun, too.

Square + Spatulate

Solid and trustworthy types, **SQUARE**s
offer the perfect steadying force for
partners with **SPATULATE** hands, whose
impulsive, impetuous nature can sometimes
get them into hot water when they act
without thinking!

Square + Conic

Well-grounded, dependable **SQUARE**s go hand in hand with partners who have **CONIC** hands, and who tend to be sensitive, spiritual souls. **SQUARE**s also have heaps of patience, which comes in useful as **CONIC**s can be overly fastidious.

Philosophical + Philosophical

The energy between you fairly crackles!
You're both intellectual, inventive and quick-
witted. You talk all night, you like the same
films, and – best of all – you really
appreciate each other's sense of humour.

Philosophical + Spatulate

Although the motto for those with **PHILOSOPHICAL** hands is 'I think' – and the motto for those with **SPATULATE** hands is 'I act' – this is still a great combination. You are both quick-witted, creative and unconventional, and you love to make each other laugh, too.

Philosophical + Conic

PHILOSOPHICALs and **CONIC**s make an unusual but frequently highly successful pairing. This is an attraction of opposites, with the logical approach of the former helping to balance the emotionally driven nature of the latter.

Spatulate + Spatulate

SPATULATEs are strong, energetic and athletic. You love to play sport, go out walking and get your hands dirty. These common threads mean that you'll have loads of interests and pastimes in common, and you'll rarely tire of each other's company.

Spatulate + Conic

The intuitive nature of those with **SPATULATE** hands is well suited to the sensitive and artistic nature of those with **CONIC** hands – you are both driven by your emotions rather than your intellect. This is a relationship with plenty of space for dreaming and creating.

Conic + Conic

Compassionate, sensitive and emotional, **CONIC**s together form a gentle and caring partnership. Because you are both led by your feelings, you are able to give each other intuitive support when things get tough. What really makes your relationship special are the unspoken messages that flow effortlessly between you.

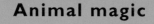

Animal magic

Chinese astrology

There are twelve signs according to
Chinese astrology, each covering an entire
year of the Chinese calendar. Each sign is
linked to a particular animal, such as the
dog, the snake and the monkey.
Use the list on the following page to see
which animal sign corresponds with your
date of birth. Then read on for details of
the most compatible combinations.

COMPATIBILITY

RAT: 15/2/72–2/2/73; 2/2/84–19/2/85

OX: 15/2/61–4/2/62; 3/2/73–22/1/74

TIGER: 5/2/62–24/1/63; 23/1/74–10/2/75

RABBIT: 25/1/63–12/2/64; 11/2/75–30/1/76

DRAGON: 13/2/64–1/2/65; 31/1/76–17/2/77

SNAKE: 2/2/65–20/1/66; 18/2/77–6/2/78

HORSE: 21/1/66–8/2/67; 7/2/78–27/1/79

GOAT: 9/2/67–29/1/68; 28/1/79–15/2/80

MONKEY: 30/1/68–16/2/69; 16/2/80–4/2/81

ROOSTER: 17/2/69–5/2/70; 5/2/81–24/1/82

DOG: 6/2/70–26/1/71; 25/1/82–12/2/83

PIG: 27/1/71–14/2/72; 13/2/83–1/2/84

Rat + Monkey

Both fun and filled with energy, you're real
party animals. With your high spirits there'll
be plenty of monkey business – just watch
out for those clashing egos. You both want
similar things from life, so pool your
energies and work as a team.

Tiger + Dog

The **DOG** offers support and protection and, in return, the **TIGER** is happy to roll over and play Tiddles in this lovable partnership, in which both respect the other's need for Me-time.

Rabbit + Goat

No kidding – you two are made for each other! You're both romantics who share every aspect of each other's life. As business partners you would do well in a venture that focuses on your creativity. What happy, rich bunnies you'd be…

Dragon + Monkey

With the **DRAGON** involved it's no surprise that this partnership is hot stuff! Your sex life will be full of animal passion and your zeal for life will keep the flames of love burning.

Snake + Rooster

You probably moved in together ten minutes after meeting! That's because you both know a good thing when you see it — and you two are definitely a good thing. Ssssorted!

Rooster + Ox

You're a practical pair who trust each other completely. The **ROOSTER** will bring out the best in the shy **OX**, while a calming environment is guaranteed when the **OX** is around.

Horse + Tiger

Giddy up for the time of your lives! You may both like to be your own boss, but your shared interests keep you rooted and randy. Neither likes to feel fenced in, though, and you both understand the other's need to do things their own way…

Goat + Goat

Billy-no-mates you're not! You two animals are a great love match with your sweet, sensitive and sensual natures. And between the two of you, your romantic leanings should keep your local florist in business.

Monkey + Dragon

You're both pleasure-seekers who like to live in the fast lane. Who cares if you have the occasional row? When your relationship's as fiery as this, it's all part of the fun.

Dog + Horse

It's lucky you're both so active, otherwise you'd wear each other out with your hectic social engagements! Variety is the spice of your lives, and you'll never get bored with each other. There's always something new to see or do!

Pig + Goat

You two will be as happy as **PIG**s in, er, clover. The **GOAT** needs a lorra, lorra love to make the relationship last, which is handy 'cos the **PIG** has plenty to give. Emotionally, it's game, set and match!

What your handwriting reveals

Graphology – the analysis of handwriting – provides a window to your inner feelings and true personality.

To analyse your handwriting – and, of course, your partner's – sit down together and copy up to 15 lines of prose from a book or magazine, and then look at your writing for its key elements. Write at your normal speed on a blank sheet of paper, using a pen you feel comfortable with.

What to look out for...

- How big is your writing, and how does it compare to your partner's in size?
- Does the handwriting slope backwards or forwards? Or is it upright? (If the slope varies, work out which direction it most frequently takes.)

Now read on and see what it all means...

Big + Big

Graphologists believe that the bigger your handwriting, the more attention and freedom you'll need to express yourself. The big–big pairing works, though, because your needs are so in tune you're able to give each other the room to be yourselves.

Big + Small

The smaller your writing, the more you tend to focus on minute issues in life. Paired with a larger writer, you're able to cover all your bases. While one of you goes off and deals with the big picture, the other focuses on getting the details right.

Small + Small

Here's a duo that never takes each other for granted! You're both attentive and careful not to upset the other, and you're both great at remembering the little things that really please each other, too. With this level of attention to detail, the big picture can take care of itself!

Forward slant + Forward slant

People whose writing slants forwards (to the right) are naturally inclined to look after their partners, come what may. When two of you come together, it's a real meeting of like-minded souls. You both work hard to make it work between you because you both believe that a successful relationship lies at the heart of a happy life.

Forward slant + Backward slant

Friendly, affectionate and extrovert, forward slanters are always looking to meet new people and draw them out of their shell. They are great soul mates for backward slanters, who tend to be more reserved, self-conscious and cautious.

Forward Slant + Upright

This is a good match because upright writers, who tend to let their head rule their heart, can't help but be swept away by a right slanter, whose loving nature puts you at the centre of their world. Write on!

Backward slant + Backward slant

Backward slanters tend to be relatively introspective, self-contained types, who need space and only form close relationships with those they feel really 'get' them. Put two of them together and you've a relationship that works because each recognizes the other's need for time alone.

Backward slant + Upright

Backward writers, often reserved and quiet types, rub along well with upright writers, who mix easily but also enjoy their own company. Adaptable and optimistic, they don't take it personally when their partner needs some space. And who doesn't?

Upright + Upright

Cool, collected and independent, upright handwriters together make for a balanced, pleasingly symmetrical combination. Neither overly outward- nor inward-looking, you both lead full lives and enjoy plenty of interests and friendships. The fun comes in sharing what you've been up to.

ABOUT CONFETTI.CO.UK

Confetti.co.uk is the UK's leading wedding and special occasion website, helping more than 100,000 brides, grooms and guests every month.

To find out more or to order your confetti.co.uk gift book or party brochure, visit www.confetti.co.uk, call 0870 840 6060, or e-mail us at info@confetti.co.uk

Other books in this series include *Men at Weddings*; *The Wedding Book of Calm*; *Wedding Readings*; *Confettiquette*; *Speeches* and the comprehensive *Wedding Planner*.

'a light-hearted
guide to relationships
and compatibility'

from  confetti.co.uk

£2.99

ISBN 1-84091-226-X